D1648942

SCYLLA AND CHARYBDIS

MONSTERS OF MYTHOLOGY

25 VOLUMES

MONSTERS OF MYTHOLOGY

SCYLLA AND CHARYBDIS

Bernard Evslin

CHELSEA HOUSE PUBLISHERS

New York   Philadelphia

1989

EDITOR
Remmel Nunn

ART DIRECTOR
Maria Epes

PICTURE RESEARCHER
Susan Quist

DESIGNER
Victoria Tomaselli

EDITORIAL ASSISTANTS
Nicole Bowen, Heather Lewis

3 5 7 9 8 6 4

Library of Congress Cataloging-in-Publication Data

Evslin, Bernard.
Scylla and Charybdis.

(Monsters of mythology)
Summary: Describes the origins of the monsters
who lived on either side of the Strait of Messina,
wreaking havoc on sailors seeking passage.
1. Scylla and Charybdis (Greek mythology)—Juvenile
literature. [1. Scylla and Charybdis (Greek
mythology) 2. Mythology, Greek] I. Title.
II. Series: Evslin, Bernard. Monsters of mythology.
BL820.S39E97   1989   398.2′1   88-18136
ISBN 1-55546-257-X
0-7910-0336-1 (pbk.)
Printed in Singapore

For my youngest grandson,
Luke Evslin,
who has learned too soon about rocks and hard places,
but will be piloted safely through

Characters

Monsters

Scylla (CIL uh)	A sea nymph studded with wolves' heads who devours sailors
Charybdis (kuh RIB dis)	A huge bladderlike creature who drinks the tides and swallows sailors
The Sphinx (SFINGKS)	Gigantic stone lioness with woman's head— deadly when she ceases to be stone
Talus (TAH los)	Bronze giant who guards the coast of Crete

Gods (Egyptian)

Buto	Cobra-goddess of the Lower Nile
Bast	Cat-goddess of the Upper Nile
Sekbet	Vulture-goddess of the Sinai
Thoth (THOHTH or TOHT)	The ibis-god — wise, kindly, and powerful

Gods (Greek)

Zeus
(ZOOS)
King of the Gods

Poseidon
(poh SY duhn)
Zeus's brother, God of the Sea

Amphitrite
(am fi TRY tee)
Poseidon's wife, Queen of the Sea

Demeter
(duh MEE tuhr)
Queen of the Harvest

Aeolus
(EE oh lus *or* ee OH lus)
God of the Wind

Alcyone
(al CY oh nee)
Aeolus's daughter

Mortals

Nisus
(NYE sus)
Prince of Egypt who practices magic

Minos
(MY nos)
King of Crete

Scylla
(CIL uh)
Wolf-girl of Corinth

Charybdis
(kuh RIB dis)
Princess of Thessaly

Daedalus
(DEHD uh luhs
or DEE duh luhs)
Great inventor and artisan who serves Minos

Ulysses
(u LIHS eez)
The greatest sea captain of antiquity

Others

Famine	Potent hag who wields hunger
The Pharaoh (FAH roe)	Father of Nisus
Amet, Crown Prince	Brother of Nisus
Two Shepherds	Parents of Scylla
Captain of Egyptian trading vessel	
Assorted Egyptians, Cretans, and Corinthians	
Wolves	
A bear	

Contents

Introduction
The Cretan Ships

Before Daedalus, ships of every kind were steered by long, heavy sweep oars pegged to their stern. But the salty old wonder-worker who had been exiled from his native Athens and given haven by King Minos of Crete replaced the great clumsy stern-oar with a hinged fin-shaped panel of bronze. He called this a *rudder*, fixed a handle to it, which became known as a *tiller*, and the ships of Minos were enabled to outmaneuver all other craft on the Middle Sea.

Daedalus also changed the rigging of the Cretan vessels so that they could tilt their sails to a quartering wind, allowing them literally to sail circles around the old-style ships which could sail only when the wind was directly abeam. And so the warships of Minos were able to defeat much larger fleets. He not only fought off the beaked ships of pirate kings who, for centuries, had harried the Cretan shores, but was able to carry the fight to the raiders' home islands.

His swift vessels fell upon the enemy like hawks upon doves. He swept the nearby waters of all who dared sail against him, and visions of empire began to dance behind his cold black eyes.

And yet, these inventions of Daedalus's that so brilliantly improved seafaring were to create a pair of monsters who wrecked so many ships and killed so many sailors that they became known as the deadliest maritime hazard of the ancient world. The way this happened is a dire and twisted tale, full of magic and mystery—the story of Scylla and Charybdis.

1

1

Shepherds and Wolves

hrough the ages, children have proven almost as useful as dogs for herding sheep. So it became the custom of shepherds to marry young and keep their wives pregnant.

Our story begins with a certain shepherd of Corinth who sired eleven sons in thirteen years and whose wife was again big with child. Both parents were awaiting the birth with great hope for they had been informed by dreams that this one would be a girl—something they had wanted for a long time. They decided to name her Scylla.

But the shepherd was never to see his daughter. Awakened by the howling of wolves upon a moonstruck night, he was patrolling a pasture with his dogs when a bush grew too tall. It became a bear rearing up on its hind legs and swept the shepherd into its fatal hug.

Bears don't eat people unless they're famished and this one was only moderately hungry. But the wolves, when they came, ate one leg before turning their attention to the sheep. And what the wolves left, the vultures finished, so that only a few gnawed bones and some bloody rags were left for the widow to burn on the funeral pyre.

She had no sooner scattered her husband's ashes than she gave birth to a daughter, and allowed herself two days to get her strength back before going out with the sheep. For the wolves were emboldened now, and were raiding the herds nightly . . . and a widow with twelve children to feed can't take time off.

In the days when humankind was new and raw and wild with delight at finally being created, the gods were sometimes aghast at what they had made. For this youngest race was noisier and more demanding by far than all the other breeds combined. So the gods grew short-tempered. The more impatient ones were quick to punish. They flailed about blindly at times, and with more force than they intended. When such rage destroyed some-one innocent this was called *accident* . . . and still is. Accidents also had a stubborn way of following certain families once they struck.

The widow had been grazing her sheep on a grassy slope.

And our shepherd family which had just lost husband and father was to suffer another loss.

The most ancient earth-goddess, Gaia, feeling herself neglected, decided to throw a mild tantrum. She shrugged her shoulders and shook a few hills in Corinth. Boulders rolled, tore up trees, hit other rocks that began to roll—and three villages were buried under landslides.

Our shepherd family dwelt beyond the farthest village, and the widow had been grazing her sheep on a grassy slope. Hearing a strange rumbling, she thrust her baby into a shallow pit—just in time. The rumbling became thunderous and a rockslide swept her away . . . her and her sheep and her dogs.

By some fluke, however, the pit mouth was unblocked, and a she-wolf, prowling in search of her cubs, which had also disappeared in the rockslide, heard a thin wailing that seemed to come out of the ground under her paws. Digging swiftly, she uncovered a human baby. The wolf was very hungry, but her udders were painfully swollen with milk, and another hunger stirred in her bereft heart. With a hoarse whine, she folded her legs, and the starving frightened baby suddenly found herself wrapped in warm fur and guzzling a wilder milk.

The she-wolf tenderly closed her jaws about the naked babe and brought her to a den dug into the slope of another hill. There the infant dwelt, suckled by the wolf, who regarded this creature as a curious unfurred cub, slow to learn, but sweet natured. And the mother wolf loved the child with a fierce protective love, and kept loving her even after the he-wolf came back to the cave.

In due time the she-wolf littered again and the baby girl found herself with three wolf-cub brothers—who, in a few weeks, could do more than she could. Two years after that, a tiny tangle-haired fleet-footed girl was flitting through the wooded slopes like a shadow—and was safer in that wild place than any child in Corinth, for she was coursing the hills with five full-grown wolves.

2

The Stone Crone

he kingdom of Corinth was a land riddled by sorcery. Its headland was dominated by a tall rock, looking out to sea. It had been sculpted by the wind into the shape of a cloaked hag, and the wind, whistling through its eyeholes, made it moan and howl. The figure became known as the Stone Crone, and was believed to be a sibyl of most ancient days whose prophecies had been so dire that she petrified herself.

People shunned the place where she stood, for they thought that whoever heard the Stone Crone speak with the wind's voice would die of fright. It was also believed that upon certain nights she awoke from her stone sleep and chased after young men, whom she crushed in her embrace.

Of all the folk in Corinth, Scylla alone did not fear the howling rock. She delighted in bringing her pack to the headland on a stormy night. The wolves would sit on their haunches, circling the cowled boulder, looking the way Scylla liked them best—the wind ruffling their feathery fur, their muzzles grinning, their eyes slits of green fire. Her wolf brothers were beautiful to her, and she nestled among them, listening to the wind singing through the rock, making the Stone Crone howl in a way that wolves understand.

A half gale blew upon this night, driving the clouds swiftly across the sky, so that the moon glittered briefly—like a blade. And Scylla, burning with excitement, feeling herself go drunk on sea-wind and moon-flash and weird song, howled back at the rock:

> Mother, demon mother,
> speak to me . . .
> Tell me, please,
> what is to be . . .

She heard the Stone Crone answer:

> Wolf-girl, wolf-girl,
> you shall stalk
> the Son of the Hawk,
> And abide the law
> of tooth and claw . . .
> First a wedding,
> then the beheading . . .

Scylla sprang up. Although not quite full-grown, she was very tall, her body suave with power. Her doeskin tunic, taken from her first kill, fell to the midpoint of her long thighs. She had never worn shoes, and her feet were hard as hooves.

Scylla sprang up. . . . Her doeskin tunic, taken from her first kill, fell to the midpoint of her long thighs.

"Thank you, Crone!" she cried. "I don't know what you mean, but it sounds wonderful."

She raced off, followed by the wolves. For the wind had shifted, had become a land-wind, bearing the smell of deer, and Scylla and her brothers were suddenly famished for meat.

3

An Egyptian Prince

Who, indeed, was this "Son of the Hawk" whose name had been uttered by the Stone Crone?

He was Nisus, an Egyptian prince, younger brother of the pharaoh, loathed by the entire court, by the priesthood, and by the military commanders—in other words, by the most potent and dangerous people in the land. Hatred of this nature is usually based on some kind of fear, and the fear of Nisus was planted before he was born. It all began when the high priest and his corps of wizards went into the desert to visit a great demon statue called the Sphinx—which was a woman's head on a lioness's crouched body, measuring a quarter of a mile from tip of nose to tip of tail.

According to legend, the Sphinx had deciphered the vital riddle of the future, and upon occasion would turn to flesh and speak to those who came to her, instructing the Egyptians on how to survive in a world growing more dangerous each day. She had not spoken now for many years, but the priests and wizards visited her at sowing time and harvest and Nile-flood, and upon the birth of every royal child. They were visiting her now as the queen went into labor.

It all began when the high priest and his corps of wizards went into the desert to visit a great demon statue called the Sphinx . . .

She had not spoken in the lifetime of anyone there, and no one really expected to hear anything on this occasion. So the assemblage of bejeweled old men were amazed when the stone cracked and fell away from the blazing body of the lioness. She arose, stretched, rippled her muscles. The empty eye sockets of the woman's head upon the lioness's body filled with cold amber light. She spoke:

"Hearken, oh priests and wizards, listen well. Children of the royal line have mortal parents, who are the pharaoh and his queen, but their ancestry stretches back to the first beast-gods of Egypt—to Ra, the Great Hawk, and to the Horned Moon whose milk is rain, known to you as Hathor, the Sacred Cow . . ."

The old men lay prostrate before the Sphinx. Their faces were pressed to the ground because the sight of her, come alive, was too terrible. And they shuddered at the sound of her voice, but sought to answer according to rote:

"Have mercy, Ra, Ra, Hawk of the Sky . . ."

"Bless us, Hathor, Sacred Cow . . ."

"Cease your monkey-chatter!" roared the Sphinx. "Be silent and heed my words!"

The crouched old men shuddered and were silent.

"A prince is about to come among you now," said the Sphinx. "He will be born tonight when the shadow of a hawk crosses the horned moon. He is a younger brother and will not rule. But he inherits more than the throne. He shall be gifted with special vision. He shall have the demigod's crystal eye that slides along the shifting cusps of Time's great spiral and *remembers* the future. He will tell you truths you are too foolish to heed, but heed them you must, or perish."

"Not perish . . ." quavered the old men. "Not that, please. Ra, Ra, have mercy now. Spare us, Hathor, Sacred Cow."

The Sphinx arose, stretched, rippled her muscles.

"Silence!" roared the Sphinx. A paw lashed out and struck a wizard, pinning him to the ground exactly as a cat pins a mouse. She drew him toward her and lifted him to her mouth. She ate him raw, wriggling, but his head went in first so his screams were muffled by the sounds of crunching.

Priests and wizards swooned in terror. When they regained consciousness, the Sphinx was stone again. She lay still, half-covered by drifting sand, as they had always seen her. And they would have thought that it had all been a dreadful dream except that one of them was missing, and the stone mouth was bloody.

Nevertheless, on their way back to the treasure-city of Rameses where their queen lay in labor, they did assure one another that it had been a dream—that they had been felled by sunstroke, as was not uncommon in the desert, and that as they lay in a swoon, their companion had wandered away, dazed, and was wandering still.

One of the wizards questioned the high priest: "Could we have all dreamed the same dream at the same time?"

"Obviously," said the high priest. "We must have. For any other notion is intolerable."

So they all publicly agreed, and secretly knew better. And

Nisus grew into a beautiful boy, lithe, gentle mannered, with a clear fearless gaze.

the words of the Sphinx rankled in them, filling them with fresh fear every time they remembered. And when little Nisus, their new prince, began to speak fluent Egyptian before he was a week old, their terror turned to hatred.

Feeling as they did, they would surely have killed the babe, except that they really believed he was descended from the Hawk and the Cow, from Isis and Osiris, and Set, the Destroyer . . . and that whoever dared harm such an infant would, himself, be snatched up by a beast-god and torn to pieces.

Nisus grew into a beautiful boy, lithe, gentle mannered, with a clear fearless gaze. His hair was as black as a night-hawk's plumage—except for a single lock that turned golden when he was about to utter a prophecy. He would be chatting of this or that, or be listening quietly, perhaps, when all at once a strand of hair would begin to glow like an ember in the middle of his head. And he would say something that horrified his elders. He would speak a simple devastating truth with no trace of impudence or of jeering—but wearing an expression almost of wonder, as if listening to what another person was saying. And indeed, it was as if something else were speaking through him.

One scribe employed by the priesthood wrote down all the child said. "I'll need a complete record of this heresy," the high priest had said. "We may find it useful one day."

One short sentence spoken by the prince was written upon a separate scroll by the scribe, and marked for special notice. It was an utterance that had aroused special hatred.

Standing on a balcony of the palace with his father, watching a victory procession, the boy felt a heat striping his head, and knew that the prophetic strand was turning to hot gold. He heard himself saying to his father:

Our triumphs are disasters . . .
Slaves shall be our masters.

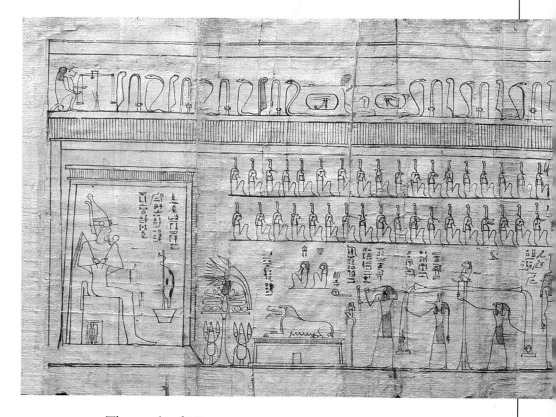

*The words of Nisus were written
down on a special scroll, to be
saved until the hour of vengeance.*

The pharaoh was not pleased to hear this, but let the displeasure slide from his mind. He was a dying man and knew that he was dying, and had resolved to let absolutely nothing trouble him.

But the high priest heard, and the scribe, and the words of Nisus were written down on a special scroll, to be saved until the hour of vengeance.

The pharaoh died soon afterward. His eldest son was too young to take the throne, so the pharaoh's brother, a silent brood-

ing man, was named regent, or temporary king, to serve until the crown prince was old enough to rule.

This heir to the throne, whose name was Ahmet, took Nisus aside and said, "Do you have any idea what's going to happen to you when I become pharaoh?"

"If you were to become pharaoh, dear Brother, I should expect dreadful things to happen to me. But since you shall never occupy the golden chair, my future is wide open."

"What do you mean I shall never be pharaoh? Are you plotting against me, you little cur? Are you forming a cabal? Fomenting sedition? I'll have your tongue torn out by the roots, your hands cut off, your eyes gouged out . . ."

"Poor Ahmet," murmured Nisus. "I'm afraid you'll have to postpone your brotherly intentions. You're in no position to command the Royal Torturers to do anything. And my prophetic insight tells me you shall never be."

Ahmet raised his ivory and ebony staff and tried to smash his brother's skull. Nisus dodged easily. "You'd be better advised to save your own life instead of trying to take mine," said Nisus. "What you should do, Prince, is bribe a shipmaster to smuggle you aboard and bear you overseas to another place."

"You'd like that, wouldn't you," cried Ahmet. "You'd like me to run off and leave you a clear road to the throne."

"You poor simpleton," said Nisus. "Neither of us is destined to rule. Do you think that sullen brute, our uncle, having held the scepter, will ever let it go? Haven't you seen the way he looks at you, hatred smoldering in his eyes? Why, he hardly bothers to conceal it. Why should he? He's used the Royal Treasury to buy half the priesthood and as much of the nobility as he needs. He's ready to make his move. Inside a week, he will instruct a shocked populace to observe a month of mourning because their crown prince has accidentally died. To demonstrate his grief he may even build a little pyramid just for you. After that, it'll be my turn because I'll be heir, but he won't find me. Brother, Brother, listen to me. You'd better dig into your treasure chest and bribe that captain."

"You're raving," snarled Ahmet. "I'm going to tell my uncle, the regent, what you've been saying."

"I'd stay away from him if I were you," said Nisus softly, but his brother was stomping away.

Nisus never saw him again. The next day, a terrible rumor flashed from mouth to ear: Ahmet was dead! Sure enough, the Grand Council was convened, and the regent solemnly announced that his beloved nephew, the pharaoh-to-be, had been bitten by a rabid monkey and had expired within the hour in a foaming fit. After decreeing a month of heavy mourning and ordering a magnificent state funeral, the regent made two other announcements: He would spend his personal fortune to build a tomb for his nephew, and he was taking immediate steps to provide for the safety of his younger nephew, Nisus, who, of course, was now heir to the throne.

But when the king's men went to search for Nisus, they found that he had vanished. The regent ordered them to ransack every corner of the kingdom, and they searched all Egypt from the Forbidden Mountain to the Red Sea but found no trace of the strange young prince.

4

Cobra and Cat

On the third night out, while sleeping on the deck, Nisus was visited by a pair of winged creatures with elongated women's bodies. Their hands and feet were talons; one had the face of a cobra, the other of a cat. They crouched on either side of him, their claws clicking on the wooden deck. He coughed and gasped in the stench of their breath, which smelled like a slaughterhouse floor. The cobra-woman spoke. Strangely, her voice was beautiful, like the wind seething among the reeds that grow on the Nile shore.

"You know us, Nisus. You have met us in your childhood, for you were prone to nightmare."

"And still am, I guess."

"No," she said. "This is not a dream. We are real, painfully real, as you shall learn."

"You are Buto," he said, "Cobra of the Lower Nile. And you, oh silent one, are Bast."

Cat-face yawned, flexing her talons.

"And you, oh failed Prince, belong to a branch of the family we detest," said Buto. "And since you are a mortal, we can safely torment you. But we shall refrain on one condition."

"Name it."

"You are a favorite disciple of Thoth. He has taught you the secret of the mandrake."

The mandrake was a plant with a forked root. When pulled from the ground, it uttered a thin cry like a newborn babe. The Delta folk believed that each plant harbored the soul of an infant born dead, and that mandrake, made into a broth and eaten by a pregnant woman, would make her bear triplets and quadruplets. So mandrake was eagerly sought by slave traders who would contract with new husbands for all the extra babes their brides could produce.

But the plant was very rare and exceedingly difficult to find without the aid of magic. And the god Thoth, he of the ibis-head, one of the few kindly gods in the Egyptian pantheon, had taught Nisus that magic. But possession of this knowledge was supposed to be a secret, and Nisus was appalled to learn that these fiends had found out.

Now, in the royal court of Egypt criminals were routinely tortured—a criminal being defined as anyone who had happened to offend the pharaoh or one of his favorites. This practice was not confined to Egypt, but it was recognized that this most ancient kingdom could boast of the world's most talented torturers, who had perfected abominations still unknown in less developed lands. . . . So Nisus, who had grown up at court, was perfectly aware of the variety of agonies that could be inflicted upon the human body. Nevertheless, he did not fear what any mortal could do to him. He knew that if the pain became unbearable he could blank himself out, cast himself into a deep coma, and slip through the portals of death where he would be safe from any man's malice.

But, for all his bravery, Nisus now found himself frozen by terror before the menace of cobra-headed Buto and cat-headed Bast. For these were gods; he could not escape them by dying. They could follow him into the cool glades of death and torment his ghost through eternity.

"Well?" hissed Buto. "Will you do as we wish?"

"Or should *we* begin doing things?" purred Bast, unsheathing her talons.

"I submit to your wishes," said Nisus. "But I must beg you to be patient. Even with the skills taught me by great Thoth, I cannot find mandrakes that aren't there. But I promise you to hunt as diligently as I can."

"We are not very patient by nature," said Buto. "But we shall grant you a certain amount of time to accomplish your task."

"No tricks!" snarled Bast. "We'll know immediately if you try to deceive us, and you will feel the full weight of our displeasure."

Hissing and yowling, they lifted themselves into the air, and the sweep of their great wings pressed a deeper darkness upon the ship as they flew away.

Nisus didn't know what to do. His whole nature forbade him to obey the beast-gods. He simply could not bring himself to produce more slaves to sate their greed. But, if he didn't . . . It was a hot night but he shuddered at the thought of what they could do to him.

He tried to cast himself into a sleep, something he could usually do. But the terror was biting too deeply; he could not sleep. So he prayed: "Oh great Thoth, wise and kindly ibis-god, instruct me now. For terrible visions have come out of the night. Buto and Bast bid me abet their crimes, and I cannot obey, and dare not refuse."

It was an ibis, royal bird of the Nile, favorite incarnation of the great Thoth.

Again, Nisus heard the sweep of great wings. He cowered to the deck, thinking that Buto and Bast had heard his prayer and were returning to punish him. Whiteness split the night, perched atop the mast. To his delight Nisus saw that it was no flying cobra or cat but an ibis, royal bird of the Nile, favorite incarnation of the great Thoth. The voice of the ibis was like the rich chuckle of the river when it ran swiftly in a narrow place. It shed peace.

"Close your eyes, Nisus," said the voice. "Sink into the realm of deeper knowledge, for I come with a countervision."

Nisus felt himself not sinking but rising into sleep. He seemed to float above the deck. A panel slid open in the profound darkness. He looked upon a radiant sward in a place he had never been. Upon that meadow grazed a herd of enormous cows, big as hippos, and graceful as horses. Their hide was pale gold, their eyes were pools of molten gold, their hooves and horns were gilded. Toward the herd over the shining grass slithered two shapes—a cobra, long as the ship's anchor line, and a cat the size of a tiger. Nisus knew that they were Buto and Bast, but wingless now.

Two cows raised their head, swished their tail, and galloped toward the invaders. The cobra rose upon its coils, its hooded head weaving, its tongue darting. The cat crouched to spring. The cows were blurs of gold as they leaped into the air. One landed upon the cobra, one upon the cat, their sharp hooves chopping. The cobra wriggled free; it was bleeding. And the cat was limping. Hissing and snarling they returned to the attack. Now the cows met them with lowered horns. They used those horns as a fencer uses his sword. One cow impaled the cobra and lifted it, writhing, into the air. The other cow drove her gilded horns straight into the cat and pinned it to the grass.

Nisus watched as the snake and the cat died. The cows withdrew their bloody horns, wiped them clean upon the grass, trotted back to the others, and began again to graze. Snake and cat vanished, then the meadow vanished. The gold slowly faded.

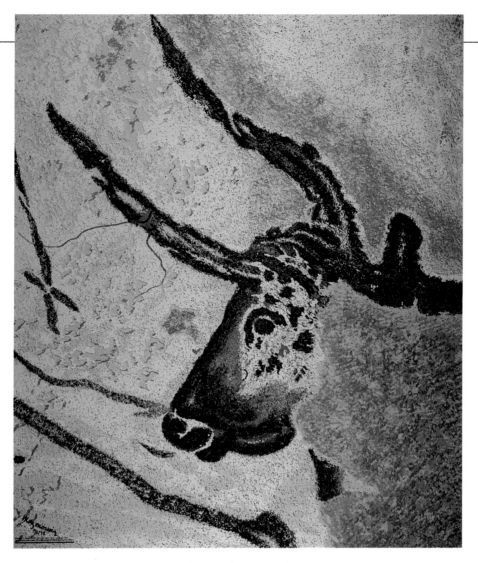

The cows were blurs of gold as they
leaped into the air. . . . They used those
horns as a fencer uses his sword.

Nisus was standing on the deck. A cool night wind bathed his fevered face. He stretched his arms to the ibis. "What does it mean?" he cried.

"It means," said the ibis, "that golden cattle are your only bulwark against Buto and Bast."

"And what does that mean?" said Nisus.

*The gold slowly faded. Nisus
was standing on the deck.*

"Buto and Bast recognize no law save their own desires,"
said the ibis. "They fear but one power, that of Hathor, the great
mother, the golden cow that rides the sky at night and whose
milk is rain. Therefore you must go to Crete and raid the unique
herds of King Minos, taking three golden cows and one golden
bull. That is the meaning of your dream. And you must take
cows and bull to the Isthmus of Corinth, for there alone grows
grass rich enough to pasture the golden cattle. You shall abide in
Corinth. Your bull will be a bull; the cows will calve; your herd

will grow. And Buto and Bast, who dread only Hathor, will view the golden cattle as a sign of her favor, and will refrain from harming you even though you defy them in the matter of the mandrake. Do you understand?"

"Not completely, my lord."

"Well, you shall learn by doing. Change the course of this vessel and sail for Crete."

"I thank you, great Thoth," cried Nisus.

The white bird uttered a rich chuckle, and his white shape split the darkness again as he flew away.

5

The Bronze Giant

When morning came, Nisus asked the captain to put about and sail for Crete. This captain, who was also the owner of ship and cargo, refused. Nisus gently repeated his wish to visit Crete.

The captain, remembering that this difficult passenger was a prince, after all, tried to bridle his temper and explained that he had no intention of changing course for the pirate-infested waters to the west. What he meant to do, he said, was skirt the coast and sail north to Phoenicia where he would trade his holdful of Egyptian cotton for Phoenician dye and cedar planks and cedar oil from Lebanon.

Even more gently, Nisus stated that it behooved the captain to change his course. For he, Nisus, promised to protect ship and cargo from all pirates, and would lead the entire company to splendid adventure and fabulous wealth.

"Even if I were inclined to believe your crazed promises," said the captain, "how do you think I could manage to sail directly against a head wind?"

"You take care of the navigation," said Nisus, "and I'll take care of the wind. I'll whistle one up that will take us right to Crete."

The vessel swung around, pointing its prow at the setting sun.

"I've heard enough," cried the captain. "Be silent immediately or I'll have you chained like a madman and set you ashore at the first landfall."

Whereupon, it is told, the amazed crew saw the prince's head catch fire. Then they realized that what they saw was a single lock of his black hair changing color, glowing red-gold. They saw him raise his hand, his fingers making horns, and point at the captain—who uttered a shriek, raced across the deck, and leaped into the water.

Nisus put his fingers to his lips and whistled. The crew heard the masts creak as the wind shifted. "Put about!" cried Nisus. They seized the lines and pulled down the huge clumsy sail, then raised it again as the bare-masted vessel swung around, pointing its prow at the setting sun.

The captain was still afloat, but soon became a speck as the ship scudded toward Crete under a freshening east wind. They still heard his screams, and knew that sharks were gathering.

King Minos summoned Daedalus to the palace and said, "I have another task for you, my artful one."

"It is my pleasure to serve you," said Daedalus, bowing low.

"I want to arrange the security of this island while my war fleet is absent—which will happen more and more frequently as I begin to attack my neighbors in a serious way. But the seas are wide. Anyone who can sail a ship is a potential enemy, and can raid us while I am invading someone else."

"What you need then," said Daedalus, "while your navy is patriotically pursuing your plans for empire, is something other than a war vessel to repel enemy shipping. Do I understand you correctly?"

"You do."

"Give me a few hours to think, Your Majesty, and I shall return with a plan, Athena willing, of course—and Hephaestus."

"Oh, I think my half brother and sister will favor our designs," said Minos, "and inspire you with another of your brilliant notions."

He spoke this way because he sought every opportunity to claim that he was a son of Zeus, something he wasn't too sure of but wished fervently to believe, and even more, to make others believe.

But whether the gods did, indeed, favor Minos, or whether imperial designs are advanced by some other agency, Daedalus was again kindled by inspiration almost divine. He created a unique sentinel for the island of Crete.

It was a statue cast in bronze, the great hollow of its thorax stuffed with springs and wheels and cogs so artfully constructed that they endowed the bronze figure with its own weird energy. Daedalus named him Talus, meaning "ankle," for the energy flowed through a veinlike channel that ran from head to foot. The vein was stoppered at the ankle by a single bronze pin. There was never a sentinel like Talus. Tall as a tree, tireless, invulnerable to weapons, he was completely obedient to the orders issued by Daedalus. He circled the island three times a day. Whenever a ship approached, he threw boulders at it, sinking it, or driving it off.

One of the under-officers approached Nisus and requested permission to speak.

"Permission granted," said Nisus, smiling at him—which confused the officer because the former captain had smiled only when about to do something cruel. This is why none of the crew had been sorry to see him go overboard.

"What I wanted to say, Your Highness, is that these waters have proved perilous of late."

"Pirates, do you mean? Why, we haven't seen a sail in days."

"No, Prince, the war galleys of Minos have swept these waters clear of pirates. And that war fleet itself is no menace to trading vessels; the Cretans are eager for trade. But Minos is away now; his ships blockade the island of Thera. And when the king sails off with his fleet, he leaves a giant patrolling the shores of Crete. He hurls boulders at any ship that approaches. He usually hits what he aims at, and what he hits, sinks."

"A single giant to patrol the entire coast?" said Nisus. "That would hardly seem sufficient."

"He's supposed to be some sort of extraordinarily magical monster, performing far beyond what flesh and blood can do."

"Well, my good man, you awaken my curiosity. I'm eager to see this unusual creature. Don't worry, though. I shan't endanger ship or crew. We'll anchor a safe distance offshore, and

I'll smuggle myself onto the island in a small boat, do what I have to do, and return to you."

"Oh my Prince," cried the man. "We have known you only a few days but we have learned to love you. Now you're proposing to throw away your life trying to do what no man can. I pray you, desist. And I know that I speak for the entire crew."

He found the cattle grazing on a meadow, and stared in admiration at the great sleek animals.

"Thank you," said Nisus. "I value what you have told me more than you can know. Still, I must ask you to have faith in me and not despair of my life. I may be a bit magical myself, you know."

Having been warned of the bronze sentinel that patrolled the Cretan coast and hurled boulders at approaching vessels, Nisus kept his ship offshore and, when night came, dived overboard and swam in.

He slept on the beach, and in the morning pushed inland, looking for the cattle. He found them grazing on a meadow, and stared in admiration at the great sleek animals, hot gold against the green grass.

He heard something and whirled about. Coming toward him was what looked like a giant in full armor. Then he saw that it was not armor. The giant *itself* was made of bronze, but moving as if alive. Nisus came to a lightning decision. He knew that he would be helpless in the grasp of that metal monster. Knew that

The giant stood stiffly on the beach.

he had only one chance—and only if he was able to reach the beach.

He needed to be on the beach because he needed sand. One of the wizardries he had learned from Thoth was the *djinn* trick of calling up a sandstorm. The ibis god had taught him a magic whirling dance that would make the sand rise in tall spouts and whirl with him. Then the spouts would go where he pointed.

He was racing through a fringe of trees toward the beach. He had chosen this route because Talus was too wide to pass between the trees and had to crash through the bush. Nevertheless, the bronze giant was enormously powerful and could cover twenty yards at a stride—and had almost caught up to Nisus before he burst out of the trees onto the beach.

Nisus immediately began to whirl. Tall spouts of sand arose and whirled also. Nisus whirled faster and faster, trying to thicken the flying sand to make himself invisible. Then, suddenly, remembering how the metal monster was constructed, he had another idea. To move the way it did, it had to be jointed at shoulder, elbow, wrist, hip, knee, and ankle. But being made of bronze and having no hide, the joints were open.

Whirling among the spouts of sand, Nisus pointed to Talus, who was groping toward him. The sand spouts moved that way and swirled about the towering figure. Nisus stopped whirling. The air cleared. The giant stood stiffly on the beach. Stiffly, creakily, it was trying to raise one massive leg. With a mighty effort it began to move toward Nisus, but rigidly, so slowly that Nisus saw that his idea had worked. Sand had settled into the metal joints, clogging them, making it almost impossible for the monster to move despite its inhuman strength.

So Nisus was able to race back to the meadow, cut out three cows and a bull, and drive them to the beach and into the sea before Talus had moved ten yards.

Nisus swam the cattle out to the ship, and heard the men cheering as he approached.

6

Prince and Wolf-girl

Scylla crouched on the brow of a hill, howling to the moon. She was very lonesome. It was spring, and the rest of the pack had paired off, leaving her to herself. She raced downhill and through the woods, over a meadow and up a steeper slope to the top of the headland which looked over the sea.

She walked toward the cliff's edge.

"No-o-o," called a cavernous voice.

She whirled about. It was the cowled boulder, the Stone Crone; her eyepits were full of moon-glare; the wind was blowing through her mouth-hole and was a voice.

"No-o-o."

Scylla faced her. "No what?"

"Don't do it. Don't jump."

"I don't want to live anymore," cried Scylla. "I'm too lonely."

"You have come into your strength. It is springtime. You need a mate."

"I can't find one. I'm too different."

"It's time you learned that," said the Crone. "You're not a wolf. You're a girl. You must find a man."

"It's time you learned . . . ," said the
Crone. "You're not a wolf. You're a girl."

"A man? Never! Good-bye. I'm going off the cliff."

"That won't solve anything."

"Why won't it?" said Scylla.

"Those who kill themselves, particularly those who are young, return as resentful ghosts who wander the earth trying to reclaim their estranged bodies. Such ghosts are the very essence of loneliness, and are condemned to wander through eternity never finding what they seek. You must try another way."

"What way?"

"Do you remember what I told you once when you asked me what was to be?"

"I remember some windy verse. I was very happy that night. I was among my brothers. It was beginning to storm. Everything was wild and beautiful."

"I'll tell you again what I told you then:

You shall stalk
the Son of the Hawk . . .

First a wedding,
then the beheading. . .

"I still don't know what that means," said Scylla.
"It means that someone is coming to Corinth—

Strong in battle,
rich in cattle. . .
He is your destiny.

"Not if he's a man," said Scylla. "I can't bear men. They're too ugly—with their bald bodies and useless noses and dull eyes and tiny teeth."

"He's not quite a man," said the Crone. "He's part wizard, as you are part wolf. He'll know how to please you."

The Crone fell silent. Scylla moved to the edge of the cliff and looked down upon the dark heaving mass of the waters. It was a long way down. Surely, such a fall would shatter even a stubborn ghost. She shuddered, backed off, turned and raced into the woods.

The next day, Scylla was prowling the edge of the forest. She hadn't eaten, but was too disheartened to stalk any game. She stiffened as the wind brought her a rich meaty smell. She followed the spoor across a meadow. In the distance she saw a blur of gold, and circled so as to conceal herself among a fringe of trees. Moving silently, blending with the shadows, she came close enough to see.

The odor was coming from three golden cows and a golden bull. Scylla hadn't realized how hungry she was. She slavered as she watched the cows. She wasn't sure she could pull one down without the help of other wolves. For these animals were enormous, and the bull was larger still; his gilded horns were sharp as spears, and he was carved of living muscle.

The bull bellowed suddenly and lowered his horns. The cows gathered in a tight group and became a hedge of horns. Scylla saw why. A bear was lumbering toward them across the meadow—a springtime bear, fresh out of hibernation, famished and foul-tempered.

A man sprang out from behind the cows and placed himself in front of the bull, facing the bear. Scylla gaped in amazement. She hadn't smelled him. He didn't quite smell like a man; he smelled of spice-wood and hot sand. He wore only a short, embroidered apron and a spiral hat. He was very slender, boyish, almost birdlike, not one to fight a beast that the mightiest hunter dared not face alone.

The bear reared up, towering over the man, prepared to take him into its fatal hug. Scylla stared at the man. Was he actually smiling, or was his face twisted by a rictus of fear? He raised his right hand and pointed at the bear. His fingertips glowed. Five streams of blue light flowed toward the bear. It whimpered and dropped to all fours—rolled over like a huge affectionate dog, waving its paws in the air. The man laughed aloud and tickled the bear's belly. The huge animal whined with pleasure.

Without conscious decision, Scylla found herself walking across the grass. She stood before him. She was much taller. Looking at his slender figure and seeing a smile kindle his face as he gazed back at her, she was swept by a desire to do what the bear had failed to do—hug him to her until she felt his ribs breaking. If he dared raise his candelabra of a hand to melt *her* will with blue flame, she would seize that arm, whirl him off his feet, smash him to the ground.

He did not raise his hand. But one lock of black hair turned red-gold. She couldn't stop herself from gasping.

"What's the matter?" he said.

"Your hair's on fire."

"No it's not."

"I see it. Some of it's burning."

"Just changing color," he said. "It's not hot. Feel . . ."

He tried to take her hand and put it on his head. She bit him. He stared at his bleeding hand in wonder, then stared at her. She was licking the blood off her lips.

"You bit me," he murmured.

"You tried to burn me."

He shook his head, a head that changed as she watched. His hair became feathers. His eyes grew huge and flared with wildness. Nose and mouth merged and solidified, became a sharp beak. It was a hawk's head he wore. Great wings sprouted from his shoulders.

"What are you doing?" she cried. "What are you?"

"A prince of Egypt," he said. "Rightful heir to a throne I shall never occupy. Nevertheless, blood is stronger than politics, and Egypt's rightful king on certain great occasions can become an earthly mode of Horus, the hawk-god."

"Can you use those wings?"

"On great occasions."

He seized her. She drew back her fist, preparing to knock him senseless—for a blow from that fist could fell a full-grown stag. But before she could strike she felt herself being lifted into the air, a feeling so delicious that she unclenched her fist and

It was a hawk's head he wore. Great
wings sprouted from his shoulders.

Sekbet was saying words above their heads.
She shadowed them with her wings.

wrapped her arm about his waist as he bore her upward through the shining air.

They were level with the cliff top now. Beyond it she could see a great blue drench of sea. Looking down over her other shoulder she saw all of Corinth beneath her, and realized for the first time that what had seemed large as the world to her was only a narrow land bridge between two landmasses.

Nisus sent a prayer eastward. "Dear Thoth, cross my flight. Appear to us and bless our marriage."

His heart thrilled as he saw a great bird coast down toward the cliff and clutch a spur of rock. He swerved in the air and headed toward the cliff, holding her more tightly. They landed on the shelf of rock, and Nisus saw that the winged one that had answered his call was not the holy white ibis but Sekbet, the vulture-headed goddess of the Sinai.

Scylla heard her hawk-man utter strange gargling words to the towering vulture-headed female, crying "Sekbet . . . Sekbet. . . ." Nisus knelt before her and pressed Scylla to earth. She felt rage growing in her, but was dazed by strangeness and did not resist.

Sekbet was saying words above their heads. She shadowed them with her wings, grasped the arm of each in her clawlike hands and lifted them to their feet. Scylla felt her face being pressed to the hawk's face. Then Sekbet flew away. Nisus balanced on the shelf of rock, watching her dwindle in the shining air. He turned to Scylla.

*He had worked a sorcery upon
        her . . . and her resentment grew.*

"We're man and wife," he said.

The words meant nothing to her. Wrapping her arm tightly about him, she crouched on her powerful legs and sprang off the rock so that he had to stretch his wings and coast on a current of air. She laughed with joy. He meant nothing to her but the wonderful new idea of flying.

Their marriage was an uneasy truce. He had taken her high and tamed her with pleasure. But when they returned to earth, when he put off his hawk's head and wings, then she resented him. He had worked a sorcery upon her, she knew. He was happy, this stranger. He was exulting because he had tamed the wolf in her. He dared to glow with a pride of ownership, and her resentment grew.

The ibis visited the prince's sleep and said: "You really can't tame a wild animal. You can cage it and bribe it and beguile it, but you must never let your attention lapse or it will turn on you and rend you."

But for the first time in life Nisus chose to ignore a warning from Thoth. He was obsessed with his big gray-eyed, leaf-smelling girl. Each time he embraced her he entered the core of mystery—felt himself touching the primal power that had formed a rubble of chaos into the garden of earth, and ignited its mud to life.

7

The Beast-gods Strike

There was a species of earth-goblin with stunted legs, shovel hands, and big yellow blunt teeth, and these misshapen creatures had proven very destructive when Egypt began. They had almost caused it to end as soon as it began because they attacked crops from underneath, pulling plants down by the roots and devouring them so greedily that they often bit their own fingers. And the people and animals were left to starve among their stripped fields—men and women and children and cattle.

They prayed for help, not really expecting any, but not knowing what else to do. But the god Thoth, always a friend to humankind, heard their prayers. He sent the goblins a collective dream; they saw a stand of delicious fat tubers growing on the slope of a certain mountain. Drunk with greed, the entire tribe came above ground and rushed to the mountain—where Thoth was waiting with a great net.

He cast the net and caught the goblins, and bore the packed screaming mass to a dead crater. He dangled the net above the crater and threatened to throw the goblins in, then hurl huge boulders down upon them. His captives screeched and wept and pleaded with him—until he agreed to spare them on one condition: that they would devour no more crops but feed only on underground herbage and earthworms. He bade them swear a mighty oath, then released them, and they scurried down the nearest hole, so frightened that they shunned ploughed fields forevermore.

Now it is not the nature of gods to accept defeat, and among the Egyptian gods, the evil ones far outnumbered the good ones, and were even more stubborn. And Buto and Bast were perhaps the most stubborn and vengeful. Thwarted in their effort to bind Nisus to their purpose, they cast about for another way to locate mandrake roots and make the Nile wives more fertile so that they might produce more babies for the slave trade.

It was a scorching day. The cat-goddess and the cobra-goddess had buried themselves up to their heads in Nile mud, trying to keep cool. Those heads were hissing and whispering to each other:

"I was thinking," said Buto. "Do you remember an ancient tale of vile little goblins who used to eat all the crops before Thoth stopped them?"

"Dimly," said Bast. "What about them?"

"I don't know," said Buto. "But I may have the glimmer of an idea. I'm going to leave you now."

"Leave this cool mud and go out under that sun? You'll regret this."

"No, I shall find a hole and slip underground. It's quite cool if you go deep enough, and I want to do a little hunting."

"Hunt what—worms?"

"Farewell," said Buto, and slithered out of the mud.

The cat-headed goddess settled herself more deeply, closed her eyes, and slept. She was awakened by a sound of weeping. A purple dusk had closed in and Buto had returned bearing something in her jaws. She set it on the ground for Bast to see. It was a squat twisted figure with bowed legs and shovel-shaped hands

Jean Dubuffet *Man Eating a Small Stone* (1944)

*The goblin wept louder than ever. . . . He
choked and coughed, and spat out the mud.*

and blunt yellow teeth. His face was writhing with fear, and he
was weeping.

"What is it?" said Bast.

"One of those goblins I was telling you about," said Buto.

"Can you make it stop that horrible blubbering?"

"You heard my friend," said Buto. "Shut up!"

*The cat-goddess said, "I tortured
him a little on the way here and
learned all the goblin secrets."*

The goblin wept louder than ever. With one hand Buto seized him by the neck, with the other she scooped up some mud and stuffed it in his mouth. He choked and coughed, and spat out the mud—and clamped his teeth tight so that he would not sob.

"That's better," said Buto. "You might as well start learning to be obedient. You're going to spend a long time serving us and any disobedience will bring much pain."

"If we must have a servant, let's get a prettier one," said Bast. "I can't bear to look at him."

"You won't have to. He'll be gone most of the time, digging up mandrake roots."

"Him?"

"Certainly," said Buto. "I tortured him a little on the way here and learned all the goblin secrets. Dwelling underground they know more about plants than anyone. Nisus may have learned the secret of the mandrake from Thoth, but these creatures were born knowing it. He'll bring us armfuls of roots every evening. We'll make him come by night so we don't have to see him. And so the pauperized Nile wives will bear many children. The slave traders will buy them and pay us a rich commission."

And it all happened that way. But success did not lull their hatred of Nisus. For among the traits that compose an evil personality is the tendency to forget friends in prosperity, but not enemies. And the cat-goddess and the cobra-goddess remembered Nisus with loathing, and often discussed what they would like to do to him if he were not protected by the magic of the golden cattle.

"We've amused ourselves by talking about that scurvy little rat long enough," said Buto. "It's time for action."

"What kind of action?" said Bast. "He's girded about with those accursed golden cattle and is immune to our direct assault."

"There's such a thing as indirect assault."

"What do you have in mind?"

"Let us fly to Corinth, you and I, and make some on-the-spot observations, what do you say?"

Bast purred agreement. They spread their wings and flew north by west over the Middle Sea.

The beast-goddesses separated when they reached Corinth, for they had agreed to divide the task—Buto to learn all she could about Nisus; Bast to pick up information about the strange girl he had married.

They met again three days later, and each knew that the other had much to tell. "You go first," said Bast.

"Well," said Buto, "it seems that our little fugitive has prospered in this place. There is a verse about him on everyone's lips; it goes like this: 'Rich in cattle, strong in battle'—for Nisus has made himself the most powerful man in Corinth. His herds have increased, and with the increase, his influence has grown. He has been able to pacify the twenty warring chieftains whose tribes were always massacring each other. Some he was able to persuade, others he vanquished on the field. In short, he imposed peace upon them, and became, in effect, king of Corinth, although he does not call himself so. The one thing he is not praised for is his marriage. His bride seems to be no one's idea of a queen."

"Aha!" cried Bast. "I have learned much about her. She's a half-savage thing, they say—raised among wolves. He practically snatched her out of her den, it seems, and forced her into marriage. Well, not forced her, perhaps, but he was able to put on the hereditary Horus form, assume hawk-head and hawk wings, and introduce her to flight. And that pleased her so much she agreed to marry him. But now, it appears, he never puts on his wings; they have virtually stopped flying, and she grows restless."

"I heard something else that may prove important," said Buto, "although it may only be rumor. It is said that Minos, king of Crete, from whom Nisus stole the golden cattle, has decided to come with an invasion fleet, reclaim his cattle, and punish Nisus. All in all, my dear Bast, the situation seems ripe for some creative mischief making."

The risen moon that night would be a hunter's moon.

"Ripe indeed," purred Bast. "And I think we should start with this wild waif he took to wife. What do you say we cook up an interesting dream for her?"

"Excellent!" cried Buto. "We'll do it this very night."

In her dream, Scylla found herself near the great roasting pit in the courtyard of the castle. The fire blazed and the flayed sheep was turning on the spit. She was very hungry, but the odor of the roasting sheep revolted her, and she knew that she would never eat cooked meat again.

Then she was on the bank of a narrow, swift river, kneeling next to a wolf that was hooking fish out of the rushing water. He was teaching her, and she was able to snatch fish out of the river with her hand, and eat them alive. And the taste of the living food was a powerful boon to her, and she knew that she must again dwell among the wolves, and shun the enclosures of humanity forevermore.

Then it was night. She was among the wolves, throbbing with joy, climbing a hill to greet the new-risen moon. For summer had gone; the air was crisp, and the wind freighted with the smell of game—and the risen moon that night would be a hunter's moon. The pack climbed to the very top of the knoll and began to call the moon to its full rise. And the howling was music to her ears.

The wind had shifted to the east now and was bringing a new smell, not of deer, but of rich beef, sleek and fat and slow of foot. She howled louder than the others and began to run down the slope, calling the pack to follow, racing to the meadow where the golden cattle grazed. She was flanked by her den brothers. She dug a hand in the ruff of each and felt herself being borne along, her feet barely skimming the earth.

She awoke from her dream. Her husband was asleep. Quiet as a shadow, she slipped out of bed and out of the chamber.

8

The Wolf Pack

isus awoke in the middle of the night to find himself alone. He hadn't heard her leave, but she could move with absolute silence when she wished. He went to an arrow-slit and looked out upon the garden. It was swimming in moonlight. He went back to bed but could not sleep.

She came with the dawn, stepping silently. He did not question her, just stared. Her nature was too direct and violent for pretense. She stood stiffly, her hands clenching and unclenching. Her eyes were glowing, her lips swollen. He saw that she was trying to subdue a profound excitement. When she spoke her voice was hoarse and clotted.

"Some nights I can't sleep. I must run beneath the moon."

"Where did you run to?"

"Nowhere. I kept within the castle grounds."

He felt his hair glowing. The chamber disappeared. He saw a moon-silvered meadow, huddled cows, shadowy shapes leaping, eyes that were pits of green fire, flashing teeth. He heard howling, snarling, the phlegmy scream of a cow in agony. He saw that cow lying on the ground, belly torn out, something dragging at its entrails.

He put on his cloak and took his spear, and without a word to his wife left the chamber. She looked after him, growling deep in her throat. She knew where he was going and what he would find.

A wolf slid into the room—a great gray male with black markings. It laid its head in her lap, then took her hand in its jaw, those jaws which could bite through the thighbone of a running stag, but which could also hold an egg without breaking the shell. She withdrew her hand and pushed the head away. She spoke to the wolf—not in shaped language as humans speak, but in grunts, yelps, whinings, faint howls. Most of it was without sound, though; she probed its eyes with hers so that her thoughts could pierce its head, and the wolf could send its thoughts back.

"Why are you here? I bade the pack leave Corinth tonight and hide in the hills beyond."

"I came to get you. We want you to come with us."

"I can't. I must stay here."

"Why?"

"You wouldn't understand. I don't understand, myself. But I must. At least for now. Leave me, Brother. Gather the pack and hasten out of Corinth to the hills beyond."

The wolf stood on its hind legs and put its forepaws on her shoulders, and licked her face. It dropped to all fours and sprang out of the room.

Tears welled from her eyes and ran down her face, but she made no sound of weeping. "They still have time," she thought. "He'll find the dead cattle and wolf tracks, but he won't be able to organize a chase until morning. By then they should be safely away. But will he know that I ran with the pack under a hunter's moon? That I did what I have longed to do for so many months? That I howled upon the hilltop and called them together—and we ran the cows as if they were deer, and, oh glory, once again I used myself as I should be used, hamstringing the first cow and bringing her down so that the others could feed? Oh, the sweet wild taste of blood in my mouth, the immense fellowship of furry shoulders pressing mine, crisp air in my lungs as I ran and ran with my brothers, and the dazzle of the low-riding moon in my eyes—Yea, the hunter's moon, lighting up our prey, but etching shadows so that we could not be seen. Such a night is worth dying for, which I well may do, if he learns that I actually hunted with the pack tonight.''

Scylla, however, had underestimated her husband's weird insight, which canceled time and abolished distance. He didn't have to visit the meadow to know what had happened to his cattle. Before leaving the castle he ordered his archers and spearmen to ride out with him on a great wolf hunt.

A wolf slid into the room—a great
gray male with black markings.

The archers launched a deadly hail of arrows.

The horses were swift, and the wolf pack, unused to fleeing anyone, traveled at a leisurely pace. The hunters caught up with the wolves as they entered a deep valley. Nisus ordered one party to ride ahead and block the outlet of the valley. He stationed another group at the valley mouth. Then he arranged his archers along the sides of the valley where they could look down upon the file of wolves trotting below.

"Now!" cried Nisus.

The archers launched a deadly hail of arrows. The spearmen rode down and drove their weapons into any wolf that was still alive. When all the wolves were dead, Nisus ordered their heads cut off. Returning to the meadow at dawn, he bade his men stick a wolf's head atop each spear and drive the hafts into the ground.

Then he galloped to the castle and asked Scylla to ride out with him. He led her to the meadow and showed her the furry heads grinning atip the spears. "This bloody palisade," he said, "will serve as a warning to all beasts who seek to ravage my herds."

Scylla did not answer. She turned her head so that he could not look into her eyes.

9

The Invasion

inos sailed against Corinth with seven hundred war vessels, each carrying thirty men-at-arms in addition to its crew. So he was able to disembark an army of twenty thousand men after an unopposed landing on the beaches of Corinth.

Everything went easily at first. He was able to secure his beachheads and move several miles inland before nightfall. Only one thing marred his satisfaction. He had seen no sign of any Corinthian. He would have preferred to have been marching over corpses; the advance would have had more reality for him—but the fishing villages were totally deserted and the few farmhouses were empty, and their fire-pits cold.

Then things changed. It was a sweltering night. Clouds hid the moon and stars, and the men had fallen into a heavy sleep. Then, suddenly, the wet darkness fledged strangers with blades— swift-moving warriors who overwhelmed the sentries, attacked the sleeping Cretans, spearing them before they could awake, killing perhaps a hundred in a very few minutes . . . and then melting into the blackness.

In the morning, Minos restored discipline by executing a few officers whom he accused of not posting enough sentries. Thereupon, he ordered an immediate advance, and the spearmen and the archers and the war chariots rolled onward in a metal wave.

But things did not go well. The invaders advanced during the day, but the night belonged to the Corinthians, whose sneak attacks continued, always with small groups of men. They continued to slip past the sentries no matter how thickly they were posted, and each time killed a certain number of Cretans. The

Daedalus had invented a new weapon—hub-knives
that whirled as the wheels turned, mowing down
the enemy like a line of farmers scything wheat.

losses were never so great as upon the first night; nevertheless, it was a steady bleeding, and Minos knew it couldn't be permitted to continue.

The Cretan king considered himself a great tactician, and indeed could boast of an unbroken string of victories. But now he felt himself thwarted. These Corinthians simply did not fight fairly. They refused to mass troops and meet him on the open field where he could use his war chariots. And he was particularly eager to use these chariots, for Daedalus had invented a new weapon—hub-knives that whirled as the wheels turned, mowing down the enemy like a line of farmers scything wheat. But without massed troops to move against, the chariots were just useless vehicles, and their horses a burden to feed.

And if the Cretans could advance across the open spaces, the Corinthians owned the forests. They knew every tree, every bush. It was death to follow them into the woods. The Cretans were sure to be ambushed. They fell into pits concealed under branches and strewn leaves; the pit bottoms were lined with sharpened stakes whose points were smeared with poison. Those who fell in died horribly. Innocent-looking trees could prove deadly too. Some of them were bent, tied down by vines, and when the vines were disturbed the tree would whip up with murderous force, squashing the armored men like beetles.

The war dragged on. The defenders took losses too, for the Cretans were brave, skillful fighters when they could manage to get within weapons' reach. Twice Minos sent his ships back to Crete for reinforcements—another forty thousand men. Finally, by sheer weight of numbers, the Corinthians were driven to the northeastern corner of the isthmus, to the city of Pagae, which Nisus had fortified.

Pagae backed upon the sea, and walls encircled it on three sides, walls of massive stone. Minos ranged his forces in an arc about the city walls, and a siege began.

One night, in the third month of the siege, Minos stood at the portal of his tent staring at the night sky, trying to read the next day's weather. The moon was out, and the stars, but there was a hazy ring about the moon, which sometimes meant rain.

He heard a rush of wings. Two enormous creatures coasted down and came to earth, one on each side of him, dwarfing him. In the bright moonlight he could see that their wings were membranous, like bat wings. One had the head of a cobra, the other of a cat. They were a frightful spectacle, but Minos had a fund of icy courage and the kind of pride that forbade him from showing fear even when he felt it. So he stopped his hand from darting to his dagger, and managed to speak calmly.

"Good evening," he said. "I've been studying the sky to see whether tomorrow will be fair or foul. What do you think?"

"Thick clouds but no rain," said the cat-headed one. Cobra-head said: "You are reputed to be a great military leader. To what do you attribute your present lack of success?"

Minos was not used to being questioned, and this question was exceedingly unpleasant. Nevertheless, as he looked at the enormous winged cobra looming above him and blotting the moonlight, he knew that he would have to answer whatever she asked.

"I asked you a question," she said. "Why are you doing so poorly in Corinth?"

"I don't know," he said. "But I've encountered a string of disasters in this accursed place. It was a bloody business getting this far. But I thought that when I had finally penned the enemy behind walls, I'd be able to finish them off. But the siege has turned sour too. My catapults are the best in the world—designed by Daedalus, you know—but for some reason they keep breaking. And when they do hurl their boulders, why the great rocks seem to turn to mud in midair and splatter harmlessly against the walls. The gods have turned against me. I can't understand it. My father is Zeus, you know."

"He has hordes of children," said Bast. "He has visited Corinth, and many of his descendants fight against you."

*As he looked at the enormous winged cobra
looming above him . . . Minos knew that he
would have to answer whatever she asked.*

"Nevertheless," said Minos, "he has always favored my designs, until now."

"Your alleged father, Zeus," said Buto, "is prone at times to play with the idea of justice—something quite alien to our Egyptian brand of god. He never allows it to interfere with his personal affairs, of course, but in spectacular, less urgent matters, like warfare, he often prefers to present the appearance of neutrality."

"True," said Minos.

"That is why your prayers for victory have met with silence."

"I don't only ask Zeus for victory," said Minos. "I pray also to my half brother, Ares, God of War."

"He can't hear you," said Bast. "He's in Persia now, a spot he favors, for truces there are as bloody as wars."

"You seem to know a lot about the affairs of the pantheon," said Minos.

"Yes," said Buto. "We gods keep track of each other, even when we operate in different territories."

"You are gods?" asked Minos.

"Goddesses. I am Buto, Cobra-goddess of the Lower Nile. My cat-faced colleague is Bast, who rules the upper stretch of the river."

"I am honored by your visit," said Minos, bowing.

"And want to know its purpose, no doubt," said Bast.

"Well . . . yes."

"We are keenly interested in your campaign, Minos. For your enemy is our enemy."

"Do you mean Nisus? I had heard that he was an Egyptian."

"A verminous specimen," hissed Buto. "And the human being we most abhor. We wish to deliver him into your hands, oh King."

"Do so, Goddess, and I shall be eternally grateful."

"Listen carefully, then. Your father, Zeus, has chosen to ignore your prayers for victory. But, perhaps, he will be moved to do you a more modest favor."

"Such as?"

"You must ask him to turn you into a wolf—just temporarily."

"A wolf? Me? Why?"

"So that you may woo your enemy's wife," said Buto. "A beautiful girl, incidentally, named Scylla."

"I don't understand."

"Pay close attention, and you will."

Whereupon Buto told him a tale that made him very thoughtful.

After the goddesses had finished their tale, and given him detailed instructions, and answered his questions, they flew away. Minos gazed after them, then spoke to the sky:

"Oh Father Zeus who put on the shape of a bull to woo my mother, Europa, please, I pray, grant me the form of a wolf for my courtship."

Lightning hooked out of the sky and touched Minos with sizzling blue flame. He disappeared. Where he had stood was a clot of darkness and two pits of light. The little king had become a huge black wolf with amber eyes. He knew he had become a wolf—but with his own intelligence and the power of speech.

"Thank you, Zeus," he cried, and loped toward the city.

He circled the walls looking for a way in. Finally, he saw a Corinthian patrol filing out of a side portal. He raced toward the wall and slid through the gate before it closed. He prowled the streets, trying to decide where Nisus dwelt. He spotted a graceful stone building inside a large garden, and leaped a low fence into the garden.

The little king had become a huge black wolf with amber eyes.

He was assailed by smells, somewhat bewildered, but delighted to discover a new sense in himself. He smelled parsley, mint, and wild asparagus; rabbit in the tall grass and an owl in a lemon tree. He lifted his muzzle and howled softly.

*He smelled someone coming. . . . her odor was a
condensation of the garden scents, lemons and mown grass.*

He waited, tasting the wind. He howled again, still softly.
He smelled someone coming—a young woman. Her odor was a
condensation of the garden scents, lemons, and mown grass. She
came straight to him. He reared up on his hind legs and put his
forepaws on her shoulders. She embraced him.

"I don't know you, Brother. Of what pack are you?"

"I suppose you would call me a lone wolf."

"You speak like a man! How is that?"

"Well, lovely girl, in another incarnation I am Minos, king
of Crete. But I have fallen in love with you, Scylla, with the kind
of love that makes all things possible. And I have put on this
form to please you."

"Oh, you do. You please me very much," murmured Scylla. "But—"

The wolf raised its paw. "I know what you're about to say—that we cannot truly belong to each other unless you become a wolf too. Well, I can manage that."

Can you?" cried Scylla. "Will you? It's my dearest wish. And if you do, I shall adore your very shadow. Can you do me now? I want to be mist-gray with black markings."

"Mist-gray," said Minos, "with black markings. It shall be done."

"Now? Right now?"

"Not quite yet. First I must have a pledge of your love."

"What kind of pledge?"

"A perilous one. A bloody one."

"I'll do anything, anything. . . . Tell me what you want."

10

Transformations

Rush torches burned in their sconces on the stone wall, making shadows dance. For Nisus never slept in darkness; he slept fully clothed, ready to spring out of bed and take command should the enemy launch a night attack.

But he was sleeping deeply now, and Scylla stood over him, studying his face. His hair was uniformly black now; the magic tress did not glow. "I'll have to cut off a lot of hair to make sure I get the right clump," she said to herself. "And he's bound to wake up. But Minos says that without that magic tress Nisus will lose his power and be easily vanquished. But he'll wake up; I know he will. It would be easier to use an axe and chop off his whole head. Yes, I'll take it to Minos and say, 'Behold my love pledge'—the head of your enemy, hair and all! And he'll be very pleased and take me to Crete. And I'll be queen and sit on a throne sometimes. But mostly we'll be wolves, as he promised, and live in a den, and run beneath the moon."

The wall was hung with weapons—swords, spears, battle-axes. She took down an axe and approached the bed. She raised the axe and held it poised. She was trying to remember the exact look of the wolves' heads stuck on the lances, trying to travel backward in time to that loathsome bloody meadow so that hatred might empower her to do this deed.

Now, axe poised, she gaped in amazement. For one lock of her husband's hair glowed golden-hot. She called on all the strength of her shoulders and arms to swing the axe and chop off his head in a single scything blow. The axe did not budge. She could not force it down. It was as if an invisible vise had clamped about it. The heavy weapon pulled itself from her hands, cleaved the air and hung itself back on the wall.

She stared after it; when she turned back, Nisus was standing before her. He spoke gently: "You don't need an axe. Your intention is enough."

She gaped at him; she couldn't speak.

"Your hatred has killed my love," he said. "And must alter me forever. You may tell Minos that your mission has succeeded. You have widowed yourself, and he can reclaim his golden cattle. But tell him also that he must not massacre the Corinthians, nor ravage the land, nor take slaves, or my vengeful ghost will torment him forever. Do you understand?"

"Yes," she whispered.

"Farewell, Scylla."

As she watched, he turned into a hawk—not a human with hawk-head and wings, but an entire hawk, a magnificent peregrine, and among the black feathers of its head sprang one gold plume.

The hawk spread its wings and flew out of the room.

Kings are not a grateful breed, and Minos was even less so. He was born to be served, he believed; others were born to serve. It was the natural order of things, and anyone in a position to do him a special service should be considered immensely privileged, and needing no further reward.

So he had no intention whatsoever of keeping his promise to Scylla. Why, he had already done much for the girl. Had changed his shape for her, spent an entire hour with her, actually vowed affection. A girl so honored should live happily the rest of her life on the rich memory.

*As she watched, he turned
into a hawk . . . spread his wings
and flew out of the room.*

"Besides," he said to himself, "I don't want to take her to Crete. She approached a domestic problem by trying to cut off her husband's head. And that sort of thing can be habit-forming. I know. I have a heavy decapitation habit myself. Is not my royal insignia the executioner's double axe? . . . So I'll rid myself of her before she gets any ideas about my own valuable head."

Whereupon he instructed the men of his guard to admit no one to his presence but members of his military staff; all strangers were to be kept away. "Especially," he said, "a big gray-eyed wench. Don't let her anywhere near."

Amphitrite worked a second transformation . . .
changing her into a sea monster—a beautiful
powerful nymph from the waist up, but six
ravening wolves below the waist.

Thus it was that after ridding herself of her husband, the young widow was truly bereaved by being denied the sight of her lover. Befuddled by passion, however, she blamed everyone but him. Blamed the Royal Guard for being overzealous in their duty. "If he knew I was out here trying to get in, he'd tell them to let me through," she said to herself.

"But there's no way to get word to him. Besides, he's busy with the truce, and withdrawing his army, and preparing the fleet. He's king and has to make all the decisions himself. No wonder he can't think of other things. But when all this damned business is wound up why then he'll come to me. He *will*. Because he loves me. I know he does. He told me so himself."

Nevertheless, when the Cretan ships departed, Scylla found herself on the beach gazing after them. In the very center of the fleet was a somewhat larger vessel with purple sails and a polished brass ram—the king's own galley. Scylla heard herself whining like an abandoned dog. She couldn't stand the sound of her voice. She dashed into the surf . . .

As it happened, the fleet was sailing before a slack wind. As Scylla began to cut through the water she saw sailors scurrying about the decks. Sails dropped, oars poked out of the row-holes. The maneuver slowed the fleet so that Scylla was able to thread among the vessels, catch up to the king's galley, and grasp its stern.

"Minos!" she screamed. "Oh Minos, my king, my wolf, my love!"

The king, standing in the bow, heard her voice. He kept his face expressionless, and did not turn his head, but barked a command. Two rowers leapt from their bench, rushed to the stern and swung their heavy oars, pounding Scylla's hands until they were bloody pulp and she could hold on no longer.

The ship sped away. She was alone in the sea, many miles from shore, and so grief stricken that she didn't even try to swim. She sank then, and would have drowned.

But Poseidon, God of the Sea, who had been watching this interesting spectacle, was so moved by Scylla's strength and beauty that he immediately made long-range plans for her, and began by changing her to a sea nymph—who could not drown. Long practice, however, had made his wife, Amphitrite, very skillful at dealing with rivals. Without hesitation, she worked a second transformation on the new Nereid, changing her into a sea monster—a beautiful powerful nymph from the waist up, but six ravening wolves below the waist.

No sooner did Scylla become a monster than all memory of her past was blotted from her mind. She lost all ability to feel or think, and knew only hunger, a raging unappeasable hunger—for human flesh.

Obeying blind instinct, she swam westward from the waters of Corinth to a much-trafficked sea-lane, the Strait of Messina, off the coast of Sicily. There she sank to the bottom and waited for a ship to pass.

11

Charybdis

emeter, Goddess of Growing Things, was furious with her nephew, Ares, Lord of Battles. Many times she had pleaded with him to refrain from fomenting his wars until the harvest was in. Often, he had agreed. But this year, a prime growing year with a rainy spring and a gentle summer, when Demeter was exulting in rich crops, Ares suddenly decided he couldn't wait an hour longer before launching a series of bloody battles.

Evenly matched armies attacked and counterattacked across the ploughed fields, trampling everything green and leaving the earth littered with corpses. So Demeter was in a foul mood as she overflew the fields in her winged chariot, observing the devastation.

She spotted something moving, and flew lower. A richly clad young woman was striding across the field, followed by two gnarled men carrying spades. Demeter kept watching them because they were headed for a certain orchard sacred to herself, which no mortal was permitted to enter.

Demeter hovered invisibly, still watching, as the young woman, whom she recognized as Charybdis, princess of Thessaly, marched into the orchard and straight up to Demeter's most

They were headed for a certain orchard. . .
which no mortal was permitted to enter.

cherished tree—one that grew the world's sweetest figs. But their chief virtue was that every fig would replace itself as soon as it was picked.

Charybdis spoke to her gardeners. "Start digging," she said. "Uproot this tree. Take it to the palace orchard and plant it there. Right outside my window, please—so that I may be able to reach out and pick the figs and eat them in bed."

The gardeners drove their spades into the earth. A wind blew through branches and became a voice, saying, "Stop . . . Stop . . ."

"Who speaks?" cried the princess.

"It is I, the dryad who dwells in this tree and is its spirit."

"And I am Charybdis, the king's daughter, to whom no one ever says 'Stop!' "

"But your gardeners must not dig me up," said the voice. "For you must know that I am sacred to Demeter, Goddess of Growing Things. No mortal is allowed to eat of my fruit, let alone transplant me."

"I am a princess," said Charybdis, "and not accustomed to denying myself anything I desire. Nor do I discuss my intentions with trees. Dig on!" she called to the gardeners.

"No, no, you don't understand. Demeter is a kindly goddess but terrible in her wrath. She will do dreadful things to you if you dare to lay impious hands on me, her favorite tree."

"Such threats do not faze me in the slightest," said Charybdis. "I don't believe in that fat old witch anyway. Nobody's actually seen her. She's nothing but an ignorant myth." She turned upon the gardeners. "You there, what are you standing around for? Dig this thing up immediately or your heads will be on the chopping block before morning."

Demeter had heard enough. She whistled up a hailstorm. It struck out of the cloudless sky; sharp chunks of ice rattled into the orchard, touching no tree, but lashing the princess and her gardeners—who fled across the field, whimpering with pain.

But Demeter's wrath was not appeased. "She's arrogant, that hussy," the goddess said to herself. "And not used to being thwarted. She'll be back with her gardeners and their spades . . . No, she won't. I'll give her something else to think about."

Whereupon Demeter returned to Olympus and sent for one of her servants. This was a dreadful servant whom she employed only when people seemed to be losing respect for the Queen of Harvests. The servant's name was Famine. She was an emaciated hag, almost a skeleton. Her flesh hung on her like rags on a scarecrow. The fleshy part of her nose was gone; her eye sockets gaped, and she had gnawed her lips away . . . so that her face was four holes and a hank of hair.

"Where have you been?" said Demeter sternly.

The servant's name was Famine. . . .
Her flesh hung on her like
rags on a scarecrow.

"In Persia, my lady, with your nephew, Ares."

"Don't talk to me about that murderous lout," cried Demeter. "Look what he's done to my crops with his damned wars."

"I don't mean to anger you, Goddess," said the hag. "But you asked me where I was and I had to tell you. I was with Ares, as my duty demanded. For Famine follows War, you know."

"Your first duty is to me."

"Yes, my lady; that's why I left Persia and hurried here at your first summons."

"Enough of this. I have a special job for you."

Charybdis awoke early the next morning. Something drew her to her window, and she gasped with pleasure. There in the orchard, twigs webbed with dew, was the fig tree she had failed to get the day before. It was stretching one branch toward her; on that branch grew a luscious fig.

"What magic is this?" murmured the princess. She had no way of knowing that the tree was a mirage planted by Demeter, and that the fig, the luscious fig was Famine itself, transformed.

Charybdis reached out, plucked the fig from the bough, and stuffed it into her mouth. It was sweet to chew; it went down smoothly. But when it hit her stomach it blossomed into hunger. More than hunger; it was a thirst, but for food. A thirst that dried every juice in her body, squeezing her entrails into one burning mandate—food!

It was early for breakfast. But roaring like a lioness, she stormed into the servants' quarters and slapped the cook awake. He gathered the other servants and rushed to the kitchen. She sat in the great dining hall, pounding on the table, roaring with impatience.

The servants came in, bearing food. A tureen big as a trough, full of porridge. An enormous ham, smoked but not sliced. Forty eggs. A barrelful of milk. She devoured it all.

"Half-rations!" she bellowed, flinging the ham bone at the cook's head. "Starvation fare! Bring food—fast!"

The cook scurried back to the kitchen and bade the under-cooks serve what had been meant for lunch. Charybdis sat in her place, pounding at the table. Her father, a small man, quite mild mannered for a king, sat staring at her in amazement—which changed to horror when the servants piled food before her and she attacked it as if she hadn't eaten for a month.

A haunch of roast ox, an immense platter, the size of a chariot wheel, loaded with barleycakes soaked in butter. A great glistening ball of cheese. Also cakes made of ground nuts and honey, and a peck of fruit.

Stupefied by food, she went back to her chamber and slept heavily . . . and awoke hungrier than ever. She charged into the dining hall, roaring for food. No one answered. The king had prudently decided that this was a good time to visit foreign lands, and had slipped away. And the servants, seeing the king go, had left also.

Silence hung over the castle. She rushed to the storeroom and studied the carcasses hanging from meat hooks. She lifted down an entire flayed sheep, sat on a keg and began to consume it. It wasn't cooked, but she didn't care. In a few hours, all the carcasses were gone, the sheep, and oxen, the dressed goats, the pigs; she had eaten them all.

She decided to take another nap before dinner. But when evening came, there wasn't a scrap of food to be found in the castle. She thought for a moment, then went out to the field where the cattle grazed.

Charybdis grew huge on her gross diet, became a giantess with a bladder of a face, keglike arms and legs, and a quadruple paunch. But for all her size she was as swift-moving as an angry sow, and usually caught whatever or whomever she was chasing. Having eaten all the livestock—cows, calves, bulls, sheep, goats, and pigs, and swept the barnyard clean of hens and chicks and roosters and ducks and geese—she had to go far afield for her meat.

She charged into the dining hall, roaring for food.

She visited farmhouses, snatched babies from their cradles, and ate them raw. And when the parents came to object, she ate them too, clothes and all—belching, and spitting buttons. The terrified people flocked to the temple of Zeus, and their prayers rose to Olympus.

Now, Zeus rarely heeded prayers. He enjoyed paeans of praise, but preferred to ignore unpleasant facts, and most prayers were complaints. Now, however, the special agony in these voices caught his attention, and he listened closely. Then seethed with rage. For he had recently passed an edict prohibiting cannibalism—with extra penalties for eating children.

He looked down and saw what Charybdis had become. He whirled her off her feet and out of Thessaly—across mountain

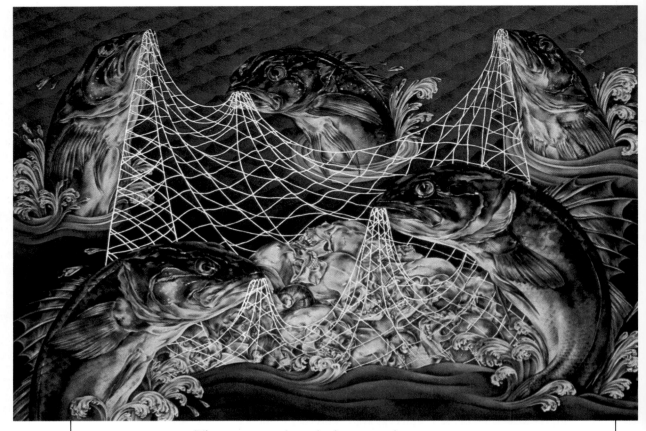

The corpses sank to the bottom and
were eaten by crabs and octopi and
other creatures who dwelt in the sea.

and plain to the sea, and westward to the Strait of Messina, where he dropped her to the bottom, just opposite the place where Scylla squatted.

He penned her in an underwater cave, saying, "Your hunger shall become thirst. As you once devoured all within reach, now you shall drink the tides twice a day. Swallow them and spit them forth, and your name shall be cursed by sailors forever."

And so it was. Twice a day, Charybdis burned with a terrible thirst and drank down the sea, shrinking the waters to a shallow stream—then spat the water out in a tremendous torrent, making a whirlpool near her rock in which no ship could live. Broken timbers floated up again and were washed onto the beaches, and became driftwood. The corpses sank to the bottom and were eaten by crabs and octopi and other creatures who dwelt in the sea.

The Strait of Messina became known as a deadly passage. But Sicily was a rich coast, and ships were sent there despite the peril. Vessels trying to steer away from the whirlpool as they passed through the strait would come too close to Scylla, who would turn her body in the water so that the wolves were uppermost. Six savage heads would sweep the deck, seizing sailors in their terrible jaws and devouring them on the spot.

And if a captain couldn't stand the idea of six great sea wolves eating his men, and steered to the left, he would feel his ship spinning like a chip as Charybdis drank the tide and drew his vessel out of sight forever . . .

12

Between Scylla and Charybdis

Ulysses was, by all accounts, the ablest captain ever to command a vessel on the Middle Sea. He was also the wiliest of the Greek battle-chiefs. He possessed absolute courage and extraordinary physical strength. All in all, he was perhaps the most resourceful hero of the ancient world. Yet, sailing home, victorious, from the Trojan War, he lost all the ships of his fleet and every man of their crews. And though he himself finally reached the shore of Ithaca, it was as a naked bleeding castaway, unrecognized, friendless, a beggar in his own kingdom.

Why did it take him ten years to make the two-month trip from Troy to Ithaca? Why so disastrous a voyage? Why so many storms, shipwrecks, fatal landfalls?

It is said that he attracted the hostility of several very vengeful gods and goddesses who spun sorceries about him and hurled monsters in his path. But why? How did this island king, reasonably pious, and worshipful of the power of the gods if not their goodness, manage to draw upon himself such a variety of divine disfavor?

The reasons are instructive, though frightening.

Some said that Ulysses had angered Poseidon by blinding his favorite Cyclopes, who had wrought gorgeous troughs for the sea-god's string of green-maned stallions. But Poseidon, al-

*It was Amphitrite, the sea-god's wife,
who sought to punish Ulysses. . . .*

though quick to wrath, was not really vengeful. He sometimes feuded with his fellow gods, but thought humans too insignificant for his full displeasure.

Rather, it was Amphitrite, the sea-god's wife, who sought to punish Ulysses, and her grudge was rooted in the way Poseidon had courted her. This joyous daughter of Oceanus had loved to frisk among the blue waves and come out at low tide to dance on the shore. Poseidon glimpsed her dancing on Naxos and fell violently in love with her. But she feared his stormy wooing and fled him to the depths of the sea. Whereupon he tried to woo her with gifts. Of coral and pearl and the bullion from sunken treasure ships he wrought her marvelous ornaments, but she spurned them all. Finally he created something entirely new for her, a talking, dancing fish. He dubbed the creature *dolphin* and sent it to Amphitrite. The dolphin pleaded Poseidon's cause with such wit and eloquence that Amphitrite yielded. She reigned as queen of the sea for many centuries, but the dolphin remained always her favorite of all creatures of the deep and she employed a string of them to pull her crystal chariot.

Now, as is told, Ulysses was the finest archer since Hercules, and kept his skill polished by practicing with his bow whenever possible. Often, during the voyage, he would try to shoot seabirds and flying fish. This kind of archery was a special challenge to him because he had to gauge the wind exactly, but he rarely missed. One day, though, while aiming at a shark, a gust of wind made his arrow swerve and pierce a dolphin—which tried one last leap and sank in a bloody froth.

Amphitrite learned about this and never forgave Ulysses. As queen of the sea she was able to strew disaster along his route— whirlpools, riptides, hidden reefs, wandering rocks. And he never learned which god was tormenting him.

But his archery was to earn him another enemy, one even more dangerous. And this mischance too was rooted in events that happened long before Ulysses was born.

Alcyone was a daughter of the wind-god, Aeolus. She married Ceyx, son of the Morning Star. They were so happy they aroused the envy of the unhappily married Hera, who sent a storm to wreck the ship on which Ceyx was voyaging. When Alcyone learned of this she drowned herself to keep him company. But Zeus pitied them and turned them into a pair of kingfishers. Each winter thereafter Aeolus forbade his winds to blow for a space of seven days so that his daughter, now a beautiful white kingfisher, could lay her eggs in a nest which floated in the sea. It is from this episode that we derive the word *halcyon*, meaning a period of calm and golden days.

But one fair morning, Ulysses detected a speck in the sky. He couldn't tell what bird it was and it seemed far out of bowshot.

But he wanted to test his prowess to the utmost. He bent his bow almost double and loosed his shaft. It flew up, up, out of sight. When it fell, it carried a white kingfisher with it. The beautiful bird sank and Ulysses' heart sank with it. Although he didn't know why, he sensed that it was unlucky to kill this creature, and that somehow he would be made to suffer for what he had done.

Fortunately for him, however, he could not possibly guess how much suffering he was to do—he and his men also. For the wind-god now loathed him totally, and his power for mischief among mariners was matchless. He sent strong head winds when Ulysses tried to sail out of port, sent savage following winds when Ulysses approached a lee shore. And, finally, cruelest trick of all, when Ulysses' ship was approaching Ithaca, coming so close the men could see the brown hills of home, Aeolus sent a gale that blew the ship hundreds of miles off its course. And it took Ulysses three years to get that close again.

Alcyone was a daughter of the wind-god, Aeolus. She married Ceyx, son of the Morning Star.

And now Aeolus decided to destroy Ulysses and his crew altogether. He sent a strong east wind that drove the ship westward toward the coast of Sicily, which was called Thrinacia at that time. Now Ulysses, master seaman that he was, always knew the location of his ship even in the grip of a storm and in darkest night. So he knew that he was approaching the Strait of Messina. Although he did not know specifically about Scylla and Cha-

*Zeus pitied the lovers and turned
them into a pair of kingfishers.*

rybdis, he had heard that the strait was a graveyard for ships. The wind was driving him too fast, he would be entering the strait before he had made a plan. He shouted to his crew, bidding them drop sail, turn the bow into the wind, and cast out the anchor.

The bare-masted ship rode the chop uneasily, but the anchor held. Ulysses paced the deck, thinking hard. A bird coasted in and landed on the deck. Not a gull, but a hawk, a huge one, with a single golden plume among the black feathers of its head.

"Hail, Ulysses," cried the hawk.

"Hail to you, whoever you are."

"I am one who has come to counsel you about your passage through the Strait of Messina."

"Indeed? I welcome any advice."

"Hearken then. Where the strait narrows, two huge rocks sit facing each other. Under each of them lurks a monster."

"Then the tales are true!" cried Ulysses. "I should have known that on this accursed voyage the worst is always true."

"Long ago," said the hawk, "in another incarnation, one of those monsters was my wife. Many years have passed since we were young and beautiful and celebrating our love in raptures of flight—many years, many murders, and many foul enchantments. I am as you see me—a hawk. And she is a sea monster, half nymph, half wolf pack, and wholly lethal. Her name is Scylla . . ."

The hawk paused. Tears dripped from his amber eyes. Ulysses stared; he had never seen a hawk weep.

"Good hawk," cried Ulysses, "tell on! I must know about these monsters."

"And I have come to instruct you, Captain. I have watched your career and learned to admire you. Also to pity you. For you, like me, have been pursued by vengeful gods and your life altered by their hatred. To resume, Scylla dwells under the right-hand rock. If you pass too close to her, six wolf-heads will sweep your deck, devouring at least six of your crew."

"Then I must steer away from Scylla—toward the other rock."

"But under the other rock lurks a thirsty monster named Charybdis who drinks the tide at one gulp, making a whirlpool that sucks down any ship within its swirl."

"Monster to the right, monster to the left! How do I sail through?"

"Keep to the middle way," said the hawk. "Exactly to the middle way, for it is not much wider than your ship. Indeed, it will be almost impossible to do unless you are sailing before a gentle wind, directly astern. If you must swerve, do it toward the right-hand rock and favor my former wife. For she will take only six or eight of your crew, but thirsty Charybdis will suck down your entire ship, drowning everyone on board."

"Thank you," said Ulysses.

Before he could finish saying it, however, the hawk had flown away.

The wind changed suddenly, and Ulysses was delighted. For it was a gentle wind now, one that would take him into the strait and push him through with sufficient leeway so that he could steer his course, keeping exactly to the middle way, avoiding both monsters.

He shouted commands. The crew leapt to their places, shipped anchor, raised the sail, and turned the bow westward toward Thrinacia.

The long oars poked out of the row-holes. . . . Scylla,
lying in wait just beneath the surface, seized two
of the oars and dragged the ship toward her.

"My thanks to you, great Aeolus," said Ulysses to the sky. "I've encountered so many contrary winds on this voyage that I was afraid I had displeased you in some way. But now I know that I enjoy your favor."

But the wind-god deserved no gratitude. The gentle wind he had sent was a piece of treachery on his part. For he wanted Ulysses to enter the strait and be destroyed that very day. Had he sent a head wind or a crosswind, Ulysses, he knew, would have sheered off and tried another time.

Ulysses suspected nothing as the ship scudded easily toward the mouth of the strait. He took the helm himself, trusting no one else to steer with the precision that was needed. The roaring of the waters grew louder and louder; he saw spray flying as Charybdis swallowed the tide and spat it back, caught a shuddering glimpse of dry seabed and gasping fish—then the tide roared back, beating itself to a white foam. He looked at the other rock. Scylla was not in sight, but she was lurking underneath, he knew, ready to spring.

The gentle wind blew. Ulysses steered his course, keeping exactly to the middle way, and they were passing through, out of reach of both monsters.

He squinted, measuring distance, then heard an appalling sound—the sails flapping. He felt the ship shudder beneath him, and yaw slightly, and knew that the wind had fallen. What he did not know was that this was Aeolus's plan: to call off the gentle east wind just when the ship was between the rocks, so that it must fall prey to one monster or the other.

"Drop sail! Start rowing," shouted Ulysses. He turned over the helm to one of the men, instructing him that if he could not keep the middle way he must veer to the right rather than to the left. Then he drew his sword and stood at the starboard rail.

The long oars poked out of the row-holes, projecting beyond the width of the hull. And Scylla, lying in wait just beneath the surface, seized two of the oars and dragged the ship toward her. Ulysses saw the polished shafts suddenly snap like twigs. The deck tilted violently. He was thrown against the rail and almost fell overboard. He picked up his sword and climbed to his feet, and saw enormous fanged heads arching over him.

He leapt toward a wolf-head and slashed at it with his sword. Its head-bones were strong as iron; he could not cut through. He reversed his sword and hammered at its teeth with his hilt. Useless. But his attack had slowed the wolves; some men were able to scurry away, but four of them were caught. He heard them screaming as they were eaten alive. Ulysses himself suffered a mangled forearm.

By then the ship had passed beyond the monster's reach. Four torn, bleeding bodies lay on deck. "Do not throw them into the sea," said Ulysses to his crew. "Mop the blood off the decks and wash the bodies of your comrades. When we make landfall we shall build them funeral pyres and dispatch their ghosts in honorable fashion."

So ended Ulysses' encounter with Scylla and Charybdis, nor when the voyage was over did he count this his worst disaster, for he had lost but four men. But the memory of the monster who was half beautiful sea nymph, half wolf pack, held a singular horror for him. He could never forget the sight of the Nereid turning gracefully in the water and becoming six pairs of savage jaws.

As for Nisus, he had suffered too much as a human ever to resume his original form. He remained a hawk and served Thoth in his ceaseless struggle against the beast-gods of Egypt.

Acknowledgments

Letter Cap Illustrations by Hrana L. Janto

Cover, SCYLLA AND CHARYBDIS *(1983/88) by Earl Staley, acrylic on canvas (47 1/2 × 63")*
   Courtesy of the artist

Op. Intro., HARBOR SCENE *(ca. 50–79 A.D.), Roman wall painting from Stabia*
   Courtesy of the Museo Nazionale, Naples
      Photo: Scala/Art Resource, NY

Page 2, WOLF *(19th century), American Indian ceremonial mask, northwest coast*
      Photo: Peter Vadnai/Art Resource, NY

Page 4, SHEEP *(1912) by Franz Marc (1880–1916) oil on canvas*
   Courtesy of the Saarland Museum, Saarbruck
      Photo: Giraudon/Art Resource, NY

Page 6, BRYCE CANYON TRANSLATION *by Max Ernst (1891–1976), oil on canvas*
   Courtesy of the Museum of Art, São Paulo
      Photo: Giraudon/Art Resource, NY

Page 8, ATALANTA *(3rd century B.C.), Roman copy of Greek original, marble*
   Courtesy of the Louvre, Paris
      Photo: Art Resource, NY

Page 10, HORUS AND PHARAOH *(ca. 1500–1000 B.C.), Egyptian wall painting from the Tomb of Seti I, Valley of the Kings*
      Photo: Beaudry/Art Resource, NY

Page 12, THE SACRED RITES OF ISIS *(ca. 80 B.C.), Roman wall painting from Herculaneum*
   Courtesy of the Museo Nazionale, Naples
      Photo: Scala/Art Resource, NY

Page 13, PALESTRINA MOSAIC *(ca. 1st century), detail depicting the Sphinx*
   Courtesy of the Museo Archeologico, Palestrina
      Photo: Scala/Art Resource, NY

Page 14, HEM-KA KNEELING IN PRAYER *(ca. 2000 B.C.), Egyptian statue*
   Courtesy of the Egyptian Museum, Cairo
      Photo: Art Resource, NY

Page 16, EGYPTIAN BOOK OF THE DEAD *(ca. 2000–1501 B.C.), papyrus scroll*
   Courtesy of the Egyptian Museum, the Vatican
        Photo: Scala/Art Resource, NY

Page 20, BLUE SLEEP *(1986) by Emilio Cruz, acrylic, pastel, and oil on paper (30 × 40")*
   Courtesy of the artist

Page 23, IBIS *(ca. 80 B.C.), wall painting from the Temple of Isis, Pompeii*
        Photo: Art Resource, NY

Page 25, COW *(ca. 15,000–10,000 B.C.), cave painting, Lascaux, France*
        Photo: Douglas Mazonowicz/Art Resource, NY

Page 26, EGYPTIAN MODEL OF A YACHT *(ca. 2000 B.C.), wood, painted and gessoed*
   Courtesy of the Metropolitan Museum of Art Excavations, 1919–20; Rogers Fund,
   supplemented by contribution of Edward S. Harkness (20.3.4)

Page 28, RIACE BRONZE *(mid-5th century B.C.), detail of head, Greek*
   Courtesy of the Reggio Calabria Archeology Museum
        Photo: Scala/Art Resource, NY

Page 30, TRAMONTO DI SOLE (SUNSET) *by Odilon Redon (1840–1916), oil on canvas*
        Photo: Scala/Art Resource

Page 33, TROOP OF CATTLE *(ca. 2500 B.C.), Egyptian sculptural relief*
        Photo: Giraudon/Art Resource, NY

Page 34, RIACE BRONZE *(mid-5th century B.C.), back view, Greek*
   Courtesy of the Reggio Calabria Archeology Museum
        Photo: Scala/Art Resource, NY

Page 36, HEAD OF A WOMAN *(ca. 6th century B.C.), Etruscan sculpture*
   Courtesy of the Vatican Museums
        Photo: Scala/Art Resource, NY

Page 38, MASK FROM A ROMAN FRESCO *(ca. 20 B.C.), villa of Augustus*
        Photo: Scala/Art Resource, NY

Page 40, BEAR *(12th century) by unknown Spanish painter, fresco transferred to canvas, from
the Church of San Baudelio de Berlanga, Soria (78 1/2 × 44 1/4")*
   Courtesy of the Metropolitan Museum of Art, The Cloisters Collection, 1957
   (57.97.4)

Page 42, GENIE *(ca. 883–859 B.C.), Assyrian limestone sculptural relief*
   Courtesy of the Louvre, Paris
        Photo: Scala/Art Resource, NY

Page 43, THE VULTURE GODDESS, *Nekhbet of Elkab, holding the "shen" sign of eternity (ca.
1490 B.C., copy of an Egyptian wall painting from the Shrine of Anubis, Temple of Hatshepsut*
   Courtesy of the Egyptian Expedition of the Metropolitan Museum of Art, Rogers
   Fund, 1930 (30.4.138)

Page 44, USERHAT KNEELS BEFORE THE FALCON-GOD RA-HARAKHTY, *symbolizing the setting
sun, and a goddess of the West (1303–1290 B.C.), copy of an Egyptian wall painting from the
Tomb of Userhat*
   Courtesy of the Egyptian expedition of the Metropolitan Museum of Art, Rogers
   Fund, 1930 (30.4.31)

Page 46, LAÖCOON *(1985) by Sam Messer, oil on linen (120 × 96")*
   Courtesy of Ruth Siegel Ltd., NY

Page 49, MAN EATING A SMALL STONE *(1944) by Jean Dubuffet (1901–1985), lithograph, (12 3/4 × 9 1/2")*
 Courtesy of the Museum of Modern Art, gift of Mr. and Mrs. Ralph F. Colin

Page 50, GODDESS *(ca. 4000 B.C.), clay figurine with reptile head*
 Courtesy of the Museum of Baghdad
  Photo: Scala/Art Resource, NY

Page 52, MOONLIT COVE *by Albert P. Ryder (1847–1917), oil on canvas*
 Courtesy of the Smithsonian Institution, Washington, D.C.
  Photo: Scala/Art Resource, NY

Page 54, HEAD OF ANUBIS *(ca. 1200–1090 B.C.), Egyptian, stuccoed wood and paint*
 Courtesy of the Louvre, Paris
  Photo: Giraudon/Art Resource

Page 57, ANUBIS *(ca. 10th–8th century B.C.), Egyptian coffin painting*
 Courtesy of the Egyptian Museum, the Vatican
  Photo: Scala/Art Resource, NY

Page 58, WAR SCENE *(710 B.C.), terra-cotta sculptural relief, Assyrian*
 Courtesy of the Museum of Baghdad
  Photo: Scala/Art Resource, NY

Page 60, WAR GALLEY *(ca. 1st century), Roman sculptural relief*
 Courtesy of the Vatican Museums
  Photo: Scala/Art Resource, NY

Page 62, CHARIOTS ARMED WITH SCYTHES *by Leonardo da Vinci (1452–1519), drawing from a sketchbook*
 Courtesy of the Bibliotek Reale, Turin
  Photo: Scala/Art Resource, NY

Page 64, DECEASED HOLDING HEART, *kneeling before winged serpent (ca. 1000 B.C.), detailed from Egyptian painting on papyrus*
 Courtesy of the Egyptian Museum, East Berlin
  Photo: Art Resource, NY

Page 67, DOGS ON A TILE FLOOR #3 *(1985) by Heidi Endemann, right panel of triptych; alkyd, charcoal, pastel, and gold leaf on paper (16 1/8 × 34 3/4")*
 Courtesy of Alexander F. Milliken Inc., NY

Page 68, ROSEBUSHES UNDER THE TREES *by Gustav Klimt (1862–1918), oil on canvas*
 Courtesy of the Musée d'Orsay, Paris
  Photo: Giraudon/Art Resource, NY

Page 70, UNTITLED *by Mark Rothko (1903–1970), watercolor, brush and ink, tempera, and pencil on paper (21 1/4 × 15 1/4")*
 Courtesy of the Metropolitan Museum of Art, Gift of The Mark Rothko Foundation, Inc., 1985 (1985.63.6)
  Photo: Lynton Gardiner

Page 73, CATACOMB NIGHTFLIGHT *(1986) by Emilio Cruz, oil on canvas (7 × 10')*
 Courtesy of the artist

Page 74, SCYLLA HURLING A BOULDER *(3rd century B.C.), Greek (Tarentine), silver emblema (diameter with frame 4 1/8")*
 Courtesy of the Metropolitan Museum of Art, Purchase, Classical Purchase and Rogers Funds, and Anonymous, Norbert Schimmel, Mr. and Mrs. Martin Fried, Mr. and Mrs. Thomas A. Spears, Walter Bareiss, and Mr. and Mrs. Howard J. Barnet Gifts, 1981 (1981.11.22)

Page 76, PORTRAIT OF A WOMAN *(ca. 1st century), Roman-Egyptian coffin painting*
Courtesy of the Archeological Museum, Florence
Photo: Scala/Art Resources

Page 78, VIEW OF A GARDEN *(ca. 20 B.C.), wall painting from the Villa of Livia at Primaporta*
Courtesy of the Museo delle Terme, Rome
Photo: Scala/Art Resource, NY

Page 80, SHE WHO WAS ONCE THE HELMET-MAKER'S BEAUTIFUL WIFE *by Auguste Rodin (1840–1917), bronze*
Courtesy of the Hirshhorn Museum & Sculpture Garden, Smithsonian Institution, Washington, D.C.
Photo: Joseph Martin/Scala/Art Resource, NY

Page 83, WOMAN WITH RAISED ARMS *by Pablo Picasso (1881–1974)*
Photo: Spadem/Art Resource, NY

Page 84, THE CATCH *(1985–86) by Heidi Endemann, watercolor and gold leaf (40 × 60")*
Courtesy of Alexander E. Milliken, Inc., NY

Page 86, STUDY, "ODYSSEUS—SCYLLA" *(1984) by Earl Staley, acrylic on paper (40 × 28")*
Courtesy of the artist

Page 88, SALTCELLAR OF FRANCIS I *by Benevenuto Cellini (1500–1571), gold with enamel (10 1/4 × 13 1/8")*
Courtesy of the Kunsthistorisches Museum, Vienna
Photo: Art Resource, NY

Page 90, THE KISS *(1908) by Gustav Klimt, oil on canvas*
Courtesy of the Osterreichisches Museum, Vienna
Photo: Bridgeman/Art Resource, NY

Page 91, LILIES, DETAIL *(ca. 1500 B.C.) fresco from Akrotiri, Thera*
Courtesy of the National Museum, Athens
Photo: Art Resource, NY

Page 93, SCYLLA AND CHARYBDIS *(1983/88) by Earl Staley, acrylic on canvas (47 1/2 × 63")*
Courtesy of the artist

BOOKS BY BERNARD EVSLIN

Merchants of Venus
Heroes, Gods and Monsters of the Greek Myths
Greeks Bearing Gifts: The Epics of Achilles and Ulysses
The Dolphin Rider
Gods, Demigods and Demons
The Green Hero
Heraclea
Signs & Wonders: Tales of the Old Testament
Hercules
Jason and the Argonauts